Breath Mark

Christy Hoff

First printing ISBN: 978-93-6354-484-0

Marshall T. Smith was the mentor who knighted me as "Poet." Ever gentle, encouraging, and edifying, Marshall passed too soon. His loss leaves a chasm of silence.

Marshall's Garden

We arrived to class curious, ready,
Fresh plowed field open to discovery.
Not knowing the path, planting, nor yield,
But trusting a gardener of truth and skill.

You laid a path of solid design,
Each brick forming a foundation line,
A platform for development, a scale true,
Words scored into our plat, seeds to grow.

You showed us the gardens of others,
Played the tunes and symphonies discovered.
Assonance, alliteration, consonance,
You respected, loved, inspired us,

Visits to the path each finding new thoughts
Sprouting new ideas, tendrils of our growth.
Encouraged by your tender nurturing,
Our basic lines became songs to sing.

Softly, as the plantings spread, we heard
A prelude drifting on assembled words.
Revealing the twittering of emotion
The humming of our creation.

Exhaling melodies of poetry,
You mentored us in mystery.
A Master orchestrating confidence
Gifting the title of poet, our acceptance.

Gone from us, your legacy remains
A symphony of poetry echoing refrains.
An elegy filled with character
In the musicality of a master.

Contents

My Creative Self

My Creative Self

Beginnings fraught with hesitation,
concentration.
Blink once, twice, bring focus to
the plane of chance.

There's fog, mist, something calling.
The direction is my choice.
What to say? What matters?
To what do I give voice?

Mist is thickening, quickening,
my heart leans into it.
Moving pencil, stirring tendrils.
Shapes come and go with the flow.

Deeply drawn, come along.
But something's in the way.
I want to see more clearly. Fearlessly.
Remove the glasses and the mask
through which they pass.

Now I'm fully placed.
Joined, one with the music of the piece.
Shape and pattern are revealed, as the meaning
is unveiled.
The shape has solidified, transmogrified.
A mirror reflecting my identity.

Breath Mark

Feet firmly planted on no-wax flooring
a whiff draws me inward.
Blinded by transcendence
I am not here.
Reaching through shoots and runners of urgency
my soul thirsts.
Today is parched.

I grasp the tendrils
of a new sprout.
Out of the fading shadows of appliances
I sense the flicker of new light
feel the warmth of a new energy
hear the introduction.

A prelude leads me away from
the ordinary
        into the verse of wonder.

Sounds of Daybreak

Dogs' tags chime a wake up call.
Splash off the mystery of last night's dreams.
Humming that keeps food fresh
stimulates a crescendo of hunger.

Rescue the teapot's ticking drum beat
before its screams wake the entire house.
Sliding door's rolling call to the fur babies.
Out – in.

The 5 beep proclamation that breakfast is ready.
Follow the morning rhythm into the living room.

Settle into the Me time of a household
-most of them-
resting.

Creak of loveseat
as pup takes up vigil at picture window.
Sigh of contentment
as loyal old friend takes the cue
relaxing full on at my feet.

Rustle of pages as I contemplate the love letter-
marching orders-forgiveness-call
of my God.
In the peace before urgency overtakes my day,
I hear hope.

Bedrock

Soft wood cannot support great resistance.
I've always been the soft wood.
My exterior a little banged up
        not the most beautiful
                a bit malleable, moldable.
Giving with pressure
        never resisting to the point of cracking.
Then gunshots set off a fire
in my town.
My heart clenched for my neighbors
        those brutalized
                those looted
                        those victimized by police
and arson.
Fear laced the sunset
        as alarms went off
                curfew was set
        National Guard rolled in.
Suddenly, a light burned the veil
        from the pathways of my beliefs.
The scent of gunpowder gave way
to remnants of smoke and fresh paint
as the strength of the community
        flowed into the wounded neighborhood.
First protection – defense
        nailed up over vulnerable openings.
A baseline of rhythm
        stroke after stroke
                the beating heart of a community
not dead.

As paint, brushes, supplies
initiate the notes of a melody
and creativity swells it
into a symphony of love.
A framework for a vantage point
Through which I can measure and analyze.
There is no room for flex or bend or
yielding.
Now that the smelting has removed the fallacy of
denial,
privilege,
ignorance
I find, resistance is necessary
to change the trajectory
of hope for equality,
for inclusive community.
Heat and pressure
are known to create diamonds
Between the piles of ash and rubble
my grey, my give, my trust was refined by
this fire.
Leaving behind a hardened resolve.
Police are not executioners.
Skin color should not be fatal.
And I have been so, so wrong...

Oz

Childhood was pictured in black and white TV,
Showing us how simple life could be.
Days were spent out of doors
with neighbors, nature, and time galore.

Walking to the bus stop, don't be late,
Dick and Jane would not wait.
I wore dresses every day
with slacks beneath so I could play.

Friends found between the covers of books
took me places and gave me hopes.
Mind's eye sees without restraint
a road, a future, without complaint.

Then came adolescence with its turbulent ways,
Signaling the end to those well patterned days.
High school leads to jobs, moves, and life goals,
A complicated picture of myself and my roles.

Full color blown in with the wind of a cyclone.

In politics, taxes, and work. Out freedom's flown.
The clear picture I'd seen was now confusing.
Friends hard to tell from those who'd abuse me.

Part of growing up is getting up each day,
facing battles and finding the yellow brick way.
Some days shivering in fear of loud commands.
Sometimes seeing the man behind the curtain.

I find myself longing for the good old days.
When I had a life in well patterned ways.
But dependence is not one of my better suits
and writing my own story is the victory I choose.

Questions

I speak into the silence
Tossing pebbles into the air
They fall with speed and little effect
Landing softly,
Sending waves in the silence
that move in my heart
I speak into the silence
tossing my cares
throwing my questions
heaving my doubts
Is there anyone to catch them?
They do not come back

Standing,
I see no one
hear nothing
Yet, the air embraces me
My heart receives
Revelations come
Directing my path
Gifts radiate
Questions answered
Revelation comes in ripples
moving my vision
shattering my fears
saturating my soul
Hope renewed
Love everlasting
A pebble lies at my feet...

Kenosha Strong

Don't miss the beauty in the midst
of pain
of fear
of destruction
of anger
of flames and foreigners.
Look deep in the heart
of my people
of painters
of cleaners
of givers
of hope.
See the *God-spirit*
in tears
in response
in caring
in standing up
and in standing with
in reaching out.
Broken people come together
to create a mosaic
to seek resolution
to lift up
to carry on.

Glitter

A gift arrived
for me!
It was packaged up so pretty.
I set it on a table
to consider thoughtfully.
I had to do my chores.
Cleaning closets, moving boxes.
But what was my gift's
Significance?

Time for bed,
day's end.
Washing up before retiring.
I see my face in the mirror,
adorned with a bit of glitter.
Rinse it off
hit the sack
tomorrow's another day.
Awaken to new momentum,
I've got a lot to say.

But first review my options.
Other gifts to exercise.
Vacuuming more glitter
managing the past.
Once again reach
nightfall,
a pinch and tiny itch.
Grope around to see I've found
more glitter on my skin!

Morning comes.
Hurray!
I'll get to it soon.
But surfing the net sends me
to a darkened room.
Distracted by the nightly news
opportunity has gone.
The gift has lost appeal,
move it to another place.

Yet, daily I find
glitter
until I'm back to it.
Bring the gift to daylight.
Free it from its wraps.
Sometimes it
fades.
The glitter shaken off.
I don't remember why it's here.
Meaning is a loss.

Other moments, I get it.
Yay!
It blooms - unfolding directly,
an obvious connection to
me, myself, and I.

Love

Look deep within the castle walls
whence the chambered maiden kept.
From blue skies tiny raindrops fall,
as deep the dragon slept.

Dare wake such malevolent beast
which knows not tempered ways.
Pray it slumbers pleased
rising not to favor chase.

The dragon knows but one pursuit,
failing that will not turn back.
But carries on till hunger met
or stronger force does wrack.

Little known to innocents.
Yea, happy their day be
dare stay among those simple guests
whose hearts remain naive.

The dragon's eyes see deep within
one's weakness to discern.
It scratches out desire hidden
leaving wounds unhealing which ever burn.

Its scales protect the true intent
with hunger ever growing.
Its strength remains unspent
till end times are foreboding.

Remember well, be warned ahead
long before torments befall.
The seeds of innocent delight
a fire-breathing menace will call.

Who dare translate this mystery
of heart and villain joined as one.
Nay even say these adverse miseries
be spread as infinity from one.

In truth the beast resides in all,
incessant in his quest
to conquer each and every one.
Leaving none to peaceful rest.

Truer still the legend heard,
the conqueror of beastly ways
who conquer wild, unruly urge
to tempered, joyful days.

Tamed and tended well
the beast will ever loyal be.
Standing fast through all and all
transformed as guardian is he.

Wisdom grows as lessons learned.
Be respectful as you go.
Tame you warily that dragon beast.
within your heart and soul.

Invocation

A new day breaks my rest,
stirs my anxious thoughts.
Lord touch my spirit and lead me in your way.
Let me be your hands in this world of solid doubt,
your feet to move through this broken world.
Let me bring your hope to the lost and the fallen.
May your wings bring protection.
May your spirit inspire my breath, lungs, and heart.
Reveal to me the gifts
you would have me send into the world.
Provide for me as you do the birds of the air and
creatures of the field.
Give me wisdom and knowledge…[1]
…make straight your way before me.[2]
...for the sake of your name lead and guide me.[3]
…may your good Spirit lead me on level ground.[4]

[1]NIV. 2 Chronicles 1:10
[2]NIV. Psalms 5:8
[3]NIV. Psalms 31: 3
[4]NIV. Psalms 143:10

Family Fruit

Family Fruit

A Sonnet

I've been digging into our family
A school project from long before you were
From a time before I met your father
Looking for ancestors, roots, and myself
Sent me spinning off to county clerk books
Triggered a cascade of overseas mail
Years tracing family trees and vices
Digging holes, searching for the mother lode
Compiling on paper, now digital
Synapses and glimpses of where we're from
Building pride and family history
On a foundation of genetic loam
A gift I've tried to pass along to you
Family future, my hope and my fruit

Roots

A Cyrch a Chwta

The bell that tolls within me
Echoes in our family,
Passed down through the centuries
Our genetic alchemy
Carried deep in each psyche.
Rhythm of this rhapsody
The echo lives on ever on
Generations' harmony.

Do not mistake the rhythm
Would ever seal out schism.
Nay, we despise in our swarm
That we hate in our own limb.
Thoughts go dark, portend a storm.
Rending home and heart in harm.
Clan and self bring on disgust
Our mind repulsed by bad form.

Lest your heart be lost in grief
Hope steals in a noisy thief
Strength of blood a ruling chief.
Forgiving in disbelief
That blood could stain our motif
Bringing back the tree in leaf.
An anchor to our life and soul
Making us whole in relief.

Coming and Going

I've come to hate my house,
without s'gettios or Legos®
        without anyone to stir the blocks.
The sound of emptiness
        can pound on the ears.

I've come to dread the going home,
without S Club 7 or singing lessons
        without burps at dinner or KPAC or Raven.
The space of an empty schedule
        can fray the nerves.

I've come to resent the piles of pulp,
on the kitchen island and the coffee table
        the litter of forgotten treasures.
The necessities buried under layers of promotion
        can sting my eyes.

I've come to understand why Great Granny
always had food to give away,
        with no one nagging, shopping is .
A relaxed pace
        can be really hard to keep.

I've come to treasure any time spent together
whether it's a visit or a text or a Facebook post,
        whether it's asking or complaining.
The love and memories we share
        can leave a residue of comfort.

Sisters: Family Tartan

The Scottish Brodie clan (my ancestry) has two tartans, one called dress and one called hunting.

We're cut from the same piece of cloth
but not in the same direction.
You are so certain of your road with no diversion
I'm happy to know wherever I go, there I am.
Are you right, cut along the lines?
Or am I okay to lean a little to the left?

Scottish clans are marked by tartan.
Double blessed, we have two choices.
You look so good no matter what,
but dress in red is truly your style.
Out in the woods or riding my bike,
I'm the hunting, mostly green.

Durable and dependable, the tartan is.
shouting loyalty in its pattern thread.
Good neighbor honest, helpful,
and willing to lend a hand.
Debts are always managed, if
only a dollar down and a dollar a week.

Roots of clover run deep,
Too the trinity is made of three.
Still one petal is left, one right,
and one more at the top.
The Lord leads our hearts,
if not our families.

The wool may itch and seem a bit rough,
can we not fire up a political conversation?
But the weave is tight to keep one warm,
are we not family when all is said and done?

Who Knew?

Who would've thought,
with the breath of nicotine
and the heat of alcohol
we would have come this far.

A needle and thread
one pulls and pushes
the other follows
leaving a trail.

The spirit-led met the devil-may-care
confused wishes for facts
and taped wings on a donkey,
called it a Pegasus.

Love designed, had a plan
without muffling the growl,
nor igniting the shadow,
but encircled, embraced the emptiness.

Who would've guessed
that two sprouts would grow
out of the maelstrom of independence,
loneliness, and co-dependence.

The branch grew shoots
and the whole tree blossomed for a time.
Caught up in the business of bearing fruit
enjoying the breath of summer
and the heat of busy-ness.

The fruit rolled off
to its own field.
The wings fell off
and darkness danced.

Steady the rhythm,
each takes a pull as the needle
sometimes the thread.

And the thread held
the pattern revealed.

Who would believe
we've made it this far.

Fall

We've a long road ahead of us.
Oh, so young and naïve,
I put you on a pedestal.
For a time you gloated, sparkled,
held your perch with pride.

But then – life – humanity.
One of us failed.
        me not holding you up?
        you not balancing carefully enough?
Each of us failed.
You
        fell.

Seeing you revealed,
knowing the truth.
There is another above us on the pedestal.
The One who belongs,
I invited you to come beside
        and worship.

You've felt left out,
wounded by the fall,
thinking I've pushed you
        off
                out,
but knowing, somehow, the Truth.

You long for the wrong position.
Trying to climb on up
        above me.

Won't you join me?
Climb the mountain called Faith.
We'll fall
        on our knees
Together.

Is Was Will

My *is* is and yours does, too
Once there was just me
                                        and you
Now me and you are not two.
Me and you are *are*.
For most of our hours.

Sometimes *are* doesn't fit so well.
My *is* chafes and yours seems to swell.
Our *are's* breath seems to catch
                                                        and comes to a stop.

Then one or the other *is* becomes
something closer to what a *we* is.
Our *are* recovers
not quite what we were
But ever after a better *will be*.

Published in the 2021 *Creative Wisconsin Anthology* as an Honorable Mention in the Wisconsin Writer's Association Jade Ring Contest

Water

Water

Consonants and vowels sprinkle onto the page
drop by drop moisten the spirit.
A sigh - a bit of relief.
Forming rivulets of meaning
more than a joining
more than multiplying
merging to become greater.
Outflow of spirit, emotion
becoming a tributary of
sorely needed release.
Storms of phrases, ideas, graces
soak bone deep into the psyche
submerging all else.
Dousing the flames of anger
embarrassment, ineptitude.
Cleansing the soul.
Immersion in the pleasure
of poetry, creation
brings new life.
Washed clean.

River

There's a river that flows, it slows, it goes, it rolls,
pushing me along.
They say water is a necessity, but this part of me,
deeper scene, living without it is impossibility.
Undeniable, indescribable, distracting path
around the bend.

Long. Oh, so long.
The river runs from a source way back in first
grade,
that fantastic, electric, eye-opening mystic
attraction for the word.
Shut my eyes, I can see it. Lines become letters,
form words become sentences, detailing
thoughts.
Waterfall! Understanding!
And I am afloat.
Carried down a stream of grammar, verbs, nouns,
phrases, hope.

Alliteration, syncopation, verbal fascination all
attempted saturation,
but there is no satisfaction for a soul that thirsts for
yet another word.
How absurd.
There are those who fight with words. Opposition
a condition of misusing and misheard.

Hidden meaning, volume screaming, others pleading.
Hearts are bleeding.
Hearts. Are. Bleeding.

Yet, there is life in fixing one more syllable in engaging links and mixing in thoughts and feelings till the whole concoction has become a flood.
Awash in understanding, a boat that carries one another to the waters that are calm.
Safe through sound, brought together, common ground, peace that wraps around.
Wound.

Wrapped in the peace that gives you ground.
Always and forever there is one that gives you ground.
Word.

Yesterday's Muse

The feeling I had yesterday
Has dulled, faded.
Like a watercolor painting
After it's been raining.
Leaving outlines
I can no longer fill.

A Bridge

I'd like to be a bridge
with one foot planted on the shores
of pain, anxiety, fear
the other on the shore of hope

It doesn't follow it will be sunshine and rainbows

But my past rests on the foundation
of so many teachers
women who've lifted me
helped me become more than I wanted to be

With enough time we'll build chords,
stretching above the rough waters.
find other truss members to fill in gaps
building strength in numbers.

The river of erosion
flows below and around
trying to saturate my confidence
wash away my strength

Stability runs through my core
iron hard certainty
that I am not alone
my skills a gift of the Creator

With an arch of wings above me
strength in the fiercest winds of opposition
support for heavy loads
present in every moment of every day

Let's be a bridge

How To Be A Poem

How To Be a Poem

1.
Is it wrong to craft
a poem in ink?
To let the words and rhythms think
they are here to stay?
Would that give them an inflated self-image?
When they are rearranged or edited out,
do they cry?

2.
Where do words go when they
are read aloud?
Does it change their trajectory whether soft
or loud, spoken flat or emoted, screeched, sung,
syncopated? Do they bring their meaning
with them or do they leave baggage behind
when
they find new partners?

3.
Is it selfish to keep a poem to
yourself?
Are they all meant to be shared or is it
wise to hide some in your own home?
Will they feel oppressed,
abused, removed?

4.
Where do poems come from? Are they born,
created, managed, or gifted? Or do they fly in
on gossamer wings? Perhaps
they simply happen, transpire,
materialize, arrive.

5.
What would I be without poems?
Would I cry?
Drag baggage with me?
Feel oppressed?
Or fly away on gossamer wings?

Genesis

I have found that certainty
is a measure of naivete.
Not having experienced the counter
        nor seen the oppressed flounder,
Finds oneself the underdog.

The way of truth is blocked constantly
        by self-absorbed philosophy.
A closed mind is an effective wall
        keeping out the threatening unknown
while creating an internal world.

I am learning to embrace the human race
        As a spectrum of kindred beings.
It's not a contest
nor a phylum of scientific selection,
but an inclusive society.

Seek outside my comfort zone
        Find folks whose ways are not my own.
Help others in any way I can
        At least try to understand
My part in humanity.

Cuyahoga

This poem is an Ae Freislighe written in ekphrasis.

A workhorse, a laborer
She sits idly waiting her turn.
Years pulling double duty.
Freight first, Passengers return.
Singing rails and air sooty
For more than 100 years.
Moving forward her concern.
Now short loop tours and kids' cheers
She sits idly waiting her turn.

Image1: "Night Train" by Gerrie Paino.

Seven: Reflecting on Snow White's 'After' Life

Waking in the forest from a sleep so deep,
New life happened, now a castle I keep.
My handsome prince, so busy ever since,
Is still the apple of my eye.

Eating apples is a problem, be wary the giver
My former life passed when it hit my liver.
Stepmothers can be mean. Cold, cruel, Queen,
Yet, I'm here and dead she be.

Fairest in the land, the title I now carry
That was mine before the prince I did marry.
Keep this palace of stone, I'm never alone
Seven little guys tug at my skirts.

Thoughts of my other seven bring tears to my eyes
Hi-ho, hi-ho, they were a brotherhood, pint-size.
Loved me, fed me, even grieved me,
Honorary dwarf, I am.

When this new life gives me no rest,
I dream of escape to the depths of the forest,
But the kiss of a prince
can otherwise convince.

PTSD: Poor Tired Sad Duck

Why did you leave me
        behind
She was terrific,
my other mother.
But she never filled
        your shadow,
                the negative space
of your absence.

She loved so much
        but not more
than her children
hated me.

How can they be so cruel?
I left the pain
only
to find
        more.
From flock to pack,
I sought peace.
Oh, to belong!
Each community,
        singing in harmony,
notes
        to a song
                I didn't know.

When will I know contentment?

At last!
        A connection with my own kind.
Their shadow matches mine,
        their song beats in my
                                        heart.
Still,
        echoes
                of yesterdays
torment,
still.

Covid Chorus

Big words, long words
Dangerous words
Scrawled deep upon our lives
Silencing the melody
We know ourselves by

Numbers panic
Rising menace
Threatens our existence
Forcing us to isolate
Tearing notes from harmony

Orders, lock down
Total quarantine
Regulating common sense
Leaders in fear
Dissonant trajectory

Our resilience
Stretched and tested
New patterns will evolve
As family reunites and
Discordant harmony resolves

Pushed

When you've been pushed to the edge of existence,
all breathing is just subsistence.
When nothing remains,
heart beating is pains,
there is only one answer.
Only one to see you through,
Jesus.

Friends and family have all moved out of the scene.
No one hears, no one
understands what you mean.
You're abandoned again,
there's no hope among men.
Only one to see you through,
Jesus.

One small flicker in the envelope of dark
One small voice
in the quiet of your heart.
You think you're sinking,
but he is uplifting.
Only one to see you through,
Jesus.

Down Clown

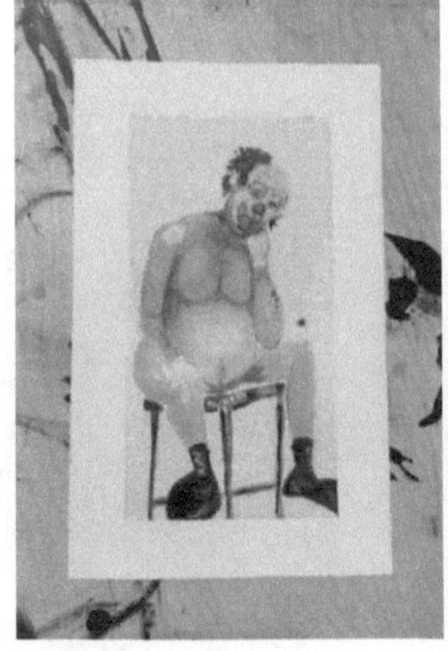

Image 2:
Kelsey Marie Harris

Why so down clown?
Turn that frown upside down.
Oh, look!
Already in the grease
upon your face
Someone tried to ease
your disgrace.
An opaque slurry of
a pancake smile.

But there it is,
You have got no spots!
No shirt, no pants,
have you forgot the lot?
Forget droopy drawers
Invisible coat of kaleidoscope colors.
No shirt or ballerina skirt.
No covering colors to generate mirth,
To hide the skin you're in,
        To hide the down of a clown,
                To hide the truth of a man.

I'd be sad, too
To sit naked like you.
Faulty, bloaty, saggy comedian
Scared, scarred, solitary sapiens
You've lost your youth!
Cover your truth!

Blackbirds of Sandy Hook

Barren swings gently sway
Gravity has won
Silence fills the day
Except the blackbirds on the playground

Silver turns to tarnish
No ascent, no thrill, no joy
Hearts instead in anguish
And the blackbirds' calls annoy

Busses pass a different way
Bells and lessons silence shroud
None dare visit on this day
But blackbirds on the playground

The Wall

Our society's issues are considered
black and white.
Just ask your neighbor, ask your sister,
ask the guy with a knife.

Ask a politician, ask a doctor,
ask a teacher.
Put their words together in a song
or a news feature.

Pile them all together and listen
for the common line.
A solid brick wall between each
speaker's what you find.

Look even closer at the mortar
filling in between.
Welding this wall tightly is the
work of one idea.

I am right – I am right –

I know the one solution.
You have a right to speak but that's
your only contribution.

Brick on brick it's built so sturdy
towering on its own.
This wall is bound surely we
may never break it down.

It's in our hand, in our fingers,
revealing our hypocrisy.
In our words, in our voice,
built so zealously.

Projected – so invective – in our
heated disquisition.
Protecting one's own ego
is our foremost mission.

But wait. Can you hear?

In the silence
pulsating is the fear.

Retune your heart and mind
find a new alignment.
Seek the common ground,
It's your new assignment.

Put away your pride,
one less brick in the wall.

Reach out to those
on the other side
to
make
it fall.

February Frustrations

Arms of trees reach up to the sky
imploring for space to spread their
branches and children.
As blade cuts deep
and rips out its roots.
Concrete planted where once the cornstalks
giggled in warm summer air.

Mausoleums of dead things
bait to the human souls
luring them away from the peace
of hard work and
dirt under their nails
to a life of
restless isolation.

Soon, fireflies will dance in the key of life
dangerously close to the tongues of the frog
croaking in the pond for all to hear.
Spending their days near the water clear
chameleon green with comfort and hope.
Bluebird sings with the chickadee
laughing at the cat stalking beneath.
Taking wing to escape, to be free
to enjoy travel far away.

Trio of deer, float silently along.
Alert! Freeze! Now dart away
pounding of heart and hooves
till deep in silence once again.

Where will the silence end?

Fractured Screen

Fractured Screen I

Formerly the family
focused on one screen,
though some disdained the *boob tube*,
together experience the same.

Discussions bloomed, debates ensued,
proving only one thing.
We all worked together
wrestling out the meaning.

Personal devices, social me-dia,
look around the room,
Each has their own device.

Separate circles splintering
the security of the nest.
Shards of past togetherness
Now severed, in the past.

Don't put your life on hold,
bring your family up.
Put them above the apps and "friends"
Who would be your current trend.

The Holy Grail

I search my world digitally
to find my importance mortally.
Yet, so much of my life goes past
ticking softly while ads distract.

Poignant saying set a meter.
My mind pulses with cloud-based fever.
Something here calls out an answer,
whose inquiry I did not engender.

My one pass in this mortal expedition
mapped step by step with insignificant decisions.
My destination seems far away
the goal diffuse, unknown today.

My purpose here is not revealed.
Yet, it calls from where it's concealed.
Gently urges, sometimes surges
waning focus when my road diverges.

Still on I search and test and hope
that I may find my breadth and scope.
In value, skill or humanity.
The holy grail my validity.

One

I lost my way
Driven to my knees
Life held captive by a virus
Fascism dictated by our ruler
Socialism bandied as a solution
Lives blasted away by our protectors
Destruction heaped on our city by foreigners
My body reminds me it is aging
My contributions are a dust mote
Drifting on the currents

That dust mote was granted me
Inbred,
Dissolved into my being
Placed for a purpose
One dot on the canvas
One pixel in the picture
One grain of sand on the path
To the One

A Hope

A sestina

Too many wires looped around my neck,
Figuratively, as they are virtual jewelry.
Flashing LED's are the gemstones of this decade.
3G, 4G, 5G where will it end?
Decades shortened to a lifespan of 3 years.
Still I cling to the hand of Father Time.

Have you seen him, Father Time?
I long to cling to his neck
To keep him near beyond his years.
Adorn him as a piece of jewelry.
Stay with him to the end,
Even if it's only this decade.

Not a native of this decade,
So often uncomfortable in this time,
I do not wish to be here at the end,
Watching civilization hang by its neck
On sordid, twisted, wired jewelry
Hardened by all these years.

Turn back the clock in years.
Go back to the bell bottom decade.
We wore natural seeds as jewelry,
Listening for the wisdom of Father Time,
Arms around each other's neck,
Instead of arms that explode into our end.

Can this really be the end?
Perhaps we can lay down arms,
Hug each other about the neck,
Bring about a new decade.
Live in peace this time.
Live up to the voice of our jewelry.

Do you wear symbolic jewelry?
Have you thought about the end?
Just who is this Father Time
Who waits with open arms?
Still alive in this decade
I long to cling to his neck.

We watch the time on our jewelry.
Rub our neck and consider the end,
Thousands of years or just this decade?

Fractured Screen II

Past scene, one screen,
Family gathered round

Snacks, tears, even fears
The tribe together found

Talk it out, cry, shout
Build Community

Sharing this experience of a single screen

Fast forward, it's today
Where did they all go?

Introverted, each alone
Splintering the home

Empty space, downward face
Only silence shared

Shards of community now a fading dream

A Psalm of Refuge

Here I sit at the mouth of the cave
Seeking the Lord my soul to save
Still I feel the cold sting of rain
Often struck by worldly pain

The Lord my rock
The Lord my hiding place
You sent your son
To lead me to grace.

Still, mocking voices cut like a knife
I bow my head 'neath the weight of life
Close my eyes to the outer world
Listen with my heart to hear God's word

One can miss the tiny spark
Deep inside, the whisper in the dark
It's important I seek
Allow his Word to shelter me

The Lord is my rock
Lord be my hiding place
I accept Your Son
To lead me to grace

Power *After Acts 8: 26-40 Phillip and the Ethiopian*

Emissary of the queen, lunar power,
who would seek the favor of any and every god,
has sent me.
The object, the oppressed, the afflicted
the shorn.
No family, no children, no hope,
nothing to call my own,
                    nothing.
The hopeless sent to secure hope.

Unsuitable, unauthorized,
despite the sparkling dew of the night,
her gold, her robes, her orders,
          her gifts.
Still, refused entrance to the Temple of God.
This sheep, lost, abandoned, enslaved,
milling with the rejected and hopeless
          straining to hear.
Parasitic questions echo,
caught up in the wool of her success.

No alternative,
following the charted course.
The moon, the stars, define the route
          back to Ethiopia.
Lured, driven back by empty promises
          good food, beautiful clothes,
to be trapped -still- in her courts.
A spark, an ember is kindled, new light rises.

Undeniable, undecipherable.
Wrestling, reading, straining to discern.
Out of the temple dust and scrolls
living words, a story so familiar.
These words are mine,
a mirror,
but how?

Comes the interpreter!
One sent by the sun intersects my path,
enlightens.
Explains how the son of the sun,
        the emissary of the God,
became a gift,
a savior.

Holy Sheep, this sheep,
same history, same fate.
Yet, my pain is His,
His pain my salvation,
        my future,
                my hope.

The Abyss

Emptiness

At the edge of the abyss,
unknown and deep,
I heave one more offering
to the god of emptiness.

My ears are filled with
the rattle of money lost
the tick
of time wasted.

Still my arms ache
with the distance of relationships faded.
My legs shake in exhaustion
burning with the effort to keep moving forward.

A beat, a hope, a river of impulses pushes,
nay, even lures me, to strive, surpass, surmount.

But, my mouth is filled with dry and bitter ashes.
The dust of wasted effort,
spent time, fruitless hope.
And so, the chasm lures.

Suddenly, I'm dancing to the staccato urgency,
frightfully close to falling in.
Books, pencils, spouse, paints, school,
children, antiques, trucks, independence, time.
All thrust at the dark, black oblivious void.
Yet, it is never full.

Giving of myself, advising, helping,
distract me from the inevitable.
Still it returns, hah, remains.

A chasm of cosmic proportions.
Exactly.
The solution is in the definition.

Fulfillment

The solution is within.
The solution is defined by *what* is within.

A spark.
Not yet warmth, but a thought.

My burning legs move, thank you.
My arms have held and hugged –
a memory that sustains.
Thank you.

And a drop of water for me.
I've felt sun on my face – joy!
The drop is joined by others,
companionship, friends, family – more joy!
Thank you.

A stream begins to flow.
Music. So grateful for hearing.
So thankful for feeling rhythm.
Appreciate a body with which to dance!

[Poem continues on next page.]

I am so small next to the chasm.
Yet, as it fills with the water
Of Life, I sense a shape.

The stream flows into the dark abyss.
Yet, reflections. Sparkles.
Thankfulness and joy reveal
the humility.

Work calls, thoughts drift and the waters calm.
Once again, I focus on the shape
of the abyss.
I see the hope
and love
and protection
it proclaims.

Social Me-dia

Your window is too small
The world view that it gives
Tainted, narrow snapshot
Blocked is all that's before
No hint of what's after
Just crumbs of a moment
So sharp they hurt the eyes
Shooting deadly poison
Mainline to heart and mind

There's no frame of reference
Bright sunlit scene seems clear
Here truth is on display
Surely your gut feeling
And kneejerk reaction
Should be allowed free reign
And will impress your friends

Reasoned debate seems dead
No courtesy, no peace
No common ground to find
Just throw your words like rocks
Then turn and shut the door
Before the slivers hit the floor.

Image 3: "Sarcofago di Stilicone" is an Ancient Roman Christian sarcophagus dating from the 4th century. It is found in Sant'Ambrogio basilica in Milan, Italy.

Ox & Ass

The relief reveals innocence
cradled between them, ox and ass.
Understood as yokes and godlessness
birds poised at each end of the image.
What are they looking for?

The people knew, regardless of literacy,
the sinless one poised between Jews and gentiles,
would come to save, bringing relief.
And here, it had already happened.

He is here, for you,
if you haven't been introduced.

A child whose purity remained.
Uncorrupt, holding to the spirit,
if not the letter,
of the law.
Clinging not to images or idols,
but living out his calling.

Today the symbols that surround us
are the elephant and the ass.
Conservative or liberal,
but there is no innocence.
Each clings to their own idol,
who are we looking out for?

Discontent

Why didn't somebody tell me,
when I was two
to find a spot
        to hold a sign
                and repeat every year.

Why didn't somebody tell me,
when I was five
to record the music I made
        repeat with every new instrument
                with each new genre.

Why didn't somebody tell me
when I was seven
to keep one souvenir rock
        from each of our family trips
                to make a mosaic of travel.

Why didn't somebody tell me
when I was ten
        to keep copies of each writing,
                each poem, each story
                        capturing me in the moment.

Something tells me
not to regret
I am the sum of these.
Each event built a life
        I carry forward
                building me.

Image References

Image 1: "Night Train" by Gerrie Paino. Rattle's Ekphrastic Challenge, April 2024.

Image 2: Kelsey Marie Harris

Image 3: File:9821 - Milano - Sant'Ambrogio - Sarcofago di Stilicone - Foto Giovanni Dall'Orto 25-Apr-2007.jpg - Wikimedia Commons. (2007, April 25).

Acknowledgements

Thank you for picking up this work and looking into my world. If it contained all the people who've helped and encouraged me it would be far too heavy to lift. But you did and I appreciate your confidence in these words to bring you to a new place.

Hours upon hours were spent refining the notes picked to compose this medley. Thank you, Samira Gdisis and Peg Roušar-Thompson for helping the rhythms and harmonies in this work become worth listening to.

My friends in the FCC Writer's Workshop, the Kenosha Writers Guild, and teachers all the way back to Miss Miller in the eighth grade all moved me forward to a place of confidence.

And never underestimate the value of family, you've supported me and I love you for it.

www.ingramcontent.com/pod-product-compliance
Lightning Source LLC
LaVergne TN
LVHW051501170726
843492LV00002B/761